# *THE LIBERATION OF THE LAITY*

## Six-Session Study Guide

and

## "Encouraging Christian Vocation in Daily Life"

Checklists

Anne Rowthorn

*Wipf and Stock Publishers*
EUGENE, OREGON

Wipf and Stock Publishers
199 West 8th Avenue, Suite 3
Eugene, Oregon 97401

The Liberation of the Laity Study Guide
Six-Session Study Guide and "Encouraging Christian Vocation in Daily Life" Checklists
By Rowthorn, Anne

ISBN: 1-59244-300-1
Publication date 7/29/2003
Previously published by Morehouse Publishing, 1993

# HOW TO USE THIS STUDY GUIDE

This study guide is designed as a straightforward means by which a group can reflect on the basic ideas presented in *The Liberation of the Laity.* It encourages participants to make personal links between the spirituality of Sunday worship and weekday ministries in the workaday world.

Each participant needs a copy of *The Liberation of the Laity* and a set of the discussion questions for each session.

Class sessions should be structured so that each participant has the opportunity to engage personally with the material. The class might be small enough to constitute one small group of between five and eight people. A larger class can be divided to form two or more small groups.

Participants should come to each session having read the assigned portions of the book.

The following format is suggested for each session:

1. First 15 minutes: silently review the reading for the session.
2. The Leader elicits brief reactions to the reading (without discussion or comment) from each member of the group.
3. The Leader passes out copies of the discussion questions for the session.
4. The Leader selects *one question* for the group to discuss. Go on to other questions as time allows.
5. Close the session with one member of the group reading a short quotation of their choosing from the assigned reading for the day.

# SESSION 1

## The Ministers of the Church

**Preparation:** Read Chapters 1 and 2, pp. 5-21.

**Discussion Questions:**

1. Who are the ministers of the Church?

2. The Chicago Declaration of Christian Concern (p. 6) states:

   In the last analysis, the Church speaks to and acts upon the world through her laity. Without a dynamic laity, conscious of its personal ministry to the world, the Church, in effect, does not speak or act.

   How do you react to this statement?

3. "You are a chosen race, a royal priesthood . . . a people claimed by God" (1 Peter 2: 9).

   What does it mean to be a member of God's royal priesthood?

   a) Who is included in this?

4. Read aloud Aristides' Letter (p. 19-20) and "The Letter to Diognetus" (pp. 20-21). These are descriptions of Christian life from the early days of "the Church Fathers."

   a) How do you respond to these two letters?

   b) How can Christians in our day be recognized in their towns and cities, and by their peers in their workplaces?

# SESSION 2

## The Liberation of the Laity

**Preparation:** Read Chapter 3, pp. 22-26.

**Discussion Questions:**

1. How do you react to the author's statement (p. 23) that:

   The quest for God begins and ends in persons. There can be no authentic search for godliness in itself; only the search for humanness, because it is in the flesh that we seek and are sought by God.

2. Do you agree that Christianity is essentially a lay movement?

3. What does the recovery of *universal lay vocation* mean to you?

4. What would the recovery of lay vocation mean to your church, and your denomination?
   a) What structural changes would need to be made?

# SESSION 3

## From Clerical Captivity Toward a Liberated Laity

Preparation: Read Chapters 4 and 5, pp. 27-51.

Discussion Questions:

1. Cite the major steps in the evolution of a clericalized Church.
2. Is there anything in the author's narrative which surprises or shocks you?
3. How is theology defined by John Macquarrie, Gustavo Gutierrez and Anne Rowthorn? (pp. 47-51)

   a) Which definition most appeals to you? Why?
4. How do you feel about Leonardo Boff's statement (p. 51) that:

   The ultimate criterion determining the truth of any and all theology is whether it produces a life of faith, hope and charity. Theology is true insofar as it is translated into meditation, prayer, conversion, the following of Christ and commitment to our fellow human beings.

# SESSION 4

## Running With the Saints

**Preparation:** Read Chapters 6 and 7, pp. 52-79.

**Discussion Questions:**

1. How does the author define Christian spirituality?
   a) What is your definition of Christian spirituality?

2. Read aloud the quotation at the bottom of p. 58 and the top of p. 59. After a moment of silence, discuss the question contained in the quotation: "Where does God himself want to be encountered by human beings?"

3. What is the role of saints in the development of each person's spiritual life?
   a) The author added Abraham Lincoln, Dorothy Day, Dag Hammarskjold, and Cesar Chavez to her list of public models of saints. Who would be included on your list? Explain your choices.

4. Silently take a few minutes to think about your personal saints who help you run your race in the pilgrimage of faith. Who are your heroes and cheerleaders? Who are those around you who make your life better, sweeter, more just? Select two of them, and with a partner, answer these questions:
   a) Why is ____________________ important to you?
   b) How does the example of ____________________ help you live your life of faith?

# SESSION 5

## Following Jesus in Everyday Life

Preparation: Read Chapters 8 and 9, pp. 80-101.

Discussion Questions:

1. Read aloud the Ecclesiasticus passage on p. 80.
   a) React to the statement that "...their prayer is in the practice of their trade."
   b) How is your everyday work within the structures of society a form of prayer?

2. With a partner, focus on your work this past week:
   a) Briefly describe your work or community activity (not your church work).
   b) Cite one situation in which you were ministered to by someone else—by a colleague, a member of the community, or perhaps a complete stranger.
   c) Still reflecting on this past week, think of a moment or a particular situation in which you reached out to a colleague, a member of the community, or a complete stranger and ministered to him or her.

3. Are there some jobs in which Christians—or anyone else for that matter—should not be engaged, because they are inconsistent with Jesus' teachings or do not contribute to the well-being of God's creation, either by what they produce, or the way goods are produced? Be specific and give examples to illustrate your points.

4. John Chrysostom, one of the early Church Fathers, said, "If we lived as the earliest Christians did, we would soon convert the whole world, with no need for miracles at all" (p. 99).
   a) Describe how the earliest Christians lived.
   b) Explain what Chrysostom was saying.
   c) Do you agree or disagree? Why?

# SESSION 6

## Awakening the Sleeping Giant

**Preparation:** Read Chapters 10 and 11, pp. 102-127.

**Discussion Questions:**

1. The author stated that:

   Worship will be authentic only inasmuch as the community of worshipers allows itself to be transformed by the servant Jesus and his cross. Liturgy will come to life to the extent that the life of this world comes to the liturgy, giving it human form, breathing into it God's breath of life. And in that liturgy is, as John Robinson has said, "the great workshop of the new world," *everything* of the life of this world, everything that converges in our personal and corporate lives must be gathered together and offered in the Eucharist (p. 107).

   a) Explain the statement.
   b) How can the worship of your congregation become a more authentic expression of the daily lives of its members?

2. How do you react to Ezekiel's image of dry bones as applied to the Church? ("Can these dry bones live?" Ezek. 37: 3)
   a) Where are your Church's dry bones?
   b) What will bring them to life?

3. In what ways does, and in what ways could, your local church strengthen and support your ministry in the workplace and in the community?
   a) What church structures and procedures need to be changed to encourage the primary ministry of the laity in the workaday world?
   b) What would you suggest as first steps?

4. What is *your* next step?

# CHECKLISTS

for

# ENCOURAGING CHRISTIAN VOCATION IN DAILY LIFE

# CHECKLISTS

## Suggestions For Congregations:

General:

1. Learn where members work and what their job responsibilities entail.

2. Find out what volunteer, civic, and community ministries parish members are involved with.

3. Discover how children and youth, the unemployed, those who are retired, homemakers, spend their time.

4. In conversation, identify parishioners primarily by their community/work/family involvements rather than by their parish roles.

5. Highlight a different parishioner and his or her lay ministry in every issue of the parish newsletter.

6. Let bulletin boards, banners, and posters reflect parishioners' occupations, vocations, and community activities.

7. Place a map of your area on a bulletin board—any road map will do. At the top attach a sign that reads "This is Where God is at Work Every Day." Invite parishioners to indicate with a cross and their initials where they spend *most* of their time during the week.

Education:

1. Form covenant groups/house churches that meet regularly in the homes of members and include in them Bible study and reflections on Christian vocation in the workplace, neighborhood, home, and community. The purpose would be: Bible study, fellowship, discernment of ministries of members, mutual support for those ministries

2. Form vocational affinity groups (lawyers, teachers, production workers, etc.) to reflect upon how faith is expressed through the ordinary channels of work and daily living. The National Center for the Laity in Chicago has produced a series of booklets in a

*Spirituality of Work* Series that could be used to facilitate the process. (Some booklets in the series include: *Lawyers, Homemakers, Teachers, Business People* and *Nurses.*) Each booklet is about 50 pages long and contains commentary by representatives of the particular occupational groups.

3. Parish education/adult forums: Have parish members take turns focusing on their work and how their faith is brought to bear in what they do, the issues they confront, the decisions they make, how they understand their daily activities as ministry.
   a) Use case studies (real ones drawn up by parish members, if possible) as a means of examining the faith/work/community connection.
   b) Study books together—non-religious books—about current social issues, and read them from a religious point of view. *Habits of the Heart,* or two of Studs Terkel's books, *Working* and *The Great Divide,* would be particularly appropriate. Current newspaper and magazine articles are useful also. (Remember that Karl Barth said that we are to read the newspaper in one hand and the Bible in the other.)

4. Invite outside guests (especially political and community leaders) to talk about their faith and work, and even to preach on occasion.

5. Parishes could consider a whole year course including elements of all the above culminating in a spring (perhaps Pentecost) liturgical celebration of all ministry, including the ministries of clergy.

## Liturgy:

1. Let the services of the gathered community encourage service in the scattered community through preaching, timely prayers, music and hymns, bulletin inserts—continually making the connection between sanctuary and street.

2. At every Sunday's liturgy, celebrate a particular line of work in which various parishioners are involved (accountants and bankers, tellers one Sunday; health care volunteers and professionals another Sunday; construction workers, building trades, and realtors another; workers on the land—farmers and ranchers; workers with children—teachers, aides, scout leaders, etc., and so on.)

a) Have workers being celebrated on a particular day bring into the liturgy symbols of their work. In preparation, ask the workers what in particular they want included in the prayers regarding their work.

3. Episcopalians: Make frequent use of "A Form of Commitment to Christian Service," *Book of Common Prayer,* p. 420, and adapt liturgies for "Lay Ministries in the Church" (Change to "Lay Ministries in the World") in the *Book of Occasional Services*, p. 160. Lutherans: Use the "Service of Affirmation of the Vocation of Christians in the World," in LBW *Occasional Service Book,* p. 147. United Church of Christ members: Adapt the "Order for Affirmation of Ministry (Installation of Lay Leaders)" in the *Book of Worship: United Church of Christ,* p. 431. Roman Catholics and others who would appreciate Stations of the Cross: Use the format in *For Those Who Work: Stations of the Cross* by Stanley J. Konieczny and Gregory Augustine Pierce.

4. Whenever parish members have job changes or promotions or are elected to political office, announce these changes publicly, congratulate them and pray for them in the Sunday service.

5. Where possible, discourage divisions between the action in the sanctuary and action in the pews. Be sure the prayers of the people are read from the heart of the congregation by a lay member. Have chalice bearers come up from the congregation at the appropriate time in street clothes to serve the communion. Laity ought to look like laity, not mini-clergy.

6. Plan a "Ministry in Daily Life" Sunday.
   a) See the leaflet, "A Sunday For Monday" (Evangelical Lutheran Church in America, Chicago, Division for Congregational Life) for suggestions.
   b) Search the hymnals of your denomination for appropriate hymns. For example, in the Lutheran Book of Worship hymns #221—"Sent Forth By God's Blessing," and #558—"Earth and All Stars," and in *Hymnal 1982,* hymns #293—"I Sing a Song of the Saints of God," and #611—"Christ the Worker." There are many others.
   c) Write a special litany specific to the lines of work and daily activities of the church members.

## Laity In Particular:

1. Help your clergy by teaching them how they can support your ministries in the world. Share with them the satisfactions, hopes, issues, conflicts, along with the regular tasks encountered in your daily life and work. Suggest concrete ways clergy can be helpful in supporting your ministries in society.

2. Invite your clergy persons to your work place and ask them to accompany you to community events you are a part of. (Clergy cannot be expected to effectively speak to and preach about the issues of your daily life unless you let them in on the important issues and routines of your daily life.)

3. Most of all, *believe* the truth that you are God's hands and feet, God's heart and mind, and God's passion for justice in this world. Believe that God's love flows through you. Believe that you really do seek and serve Christ in every person you encounter. Then you will see that every moment in your life and every encounter you have with other human beings has significance. Really believing in the depth of your being that God is alive in you and in others will affect everything you do.

## Clergy In Particular:

1. Inform yourself about where your parish members work. What are their joys, successes, and accomplishments? What issues confront them at their work places (including the conflicts and possible ethical issues of their employment)?

2. For members who are retired or full time volunteers, find out how they spend their time and what they are doing now that they did not have time for when they were working.

3. Whenever possible hold lunchtime or late afternoon meetings in parishioners' work places rather than in parish buildings.

4. Take a day every two weeks to go to work with members of your parish in order to see for yourself a little of their daily lifestyle/work.

5. Visit members who are active in politics and public life in their public settings and find out how their participation is an expression of their faith.

6. Laity must struggle to make creative connections between the relationship of Sunday to Monday. You will increase your effectiveness as a pastor and preacher as you stand beside them while they seek to make these critical connections in their lives. First put yourself in their shoes, and then begin writing your sermon. Use your sermons to reflect upon the connections between daily life and faith. Let the daily lives and work of church members provide the illustrations you use in your sermons.

## Questions For Bishops And Denominational Leaders:

1. Are lay persons sufficiently present as part of important denominational and ecumenical committees and commissions? Are they strong, vibrant laity with a lively sense of their own important ministries in the world? And when they are represented, are their experience, opinions, and contributions as valued as those of the clergy?

2. Are there any denominational structures or procedures which prevent lay participation?

3. Are professional lay workers included in denominational leadership conferences, or are such occasions for clergy only? When they have similar or parallel qualifications, are they receiving equal salary and benefits with the clergy?

4. What is the reward system in your denomination? Is the Christian who is an honest, altruistic realtor or local politician given as much recognition in your church, in denominational newsletters and such, as General Convention, Conference and Synod delegates?

5. Is your denomination's Commission on Ministry really the Commission on the Ordained Ministry?

6. Does your denomination have a Commission on the Ministry of the Laity with equal status and funding as the Commission on Ministry?

7. In denominational publications, are the laity cited the same way as clergy: Mrs., Mr., Dr., Ms., for laity to balance the Rev. in front of the cleric's name? In meeting reports are clergy and laity listed alphabetically, or are clergy listed first?

8. How does your denomination handle serious and devout calls to ministry except to suggest ordination?

# FURTHER STUDY


## Biblical and Theological Foundations

Boff, Leonardo, *Jesus Christ Liberator: A Critical Christology for Our Time.* Tr. by Patrick Hughes. Maryknoll, NY: Orbis Books, 1978.

Kraemer, Hendrick, *A Theology of the Laity.* Philadelphia: Westminster Press, 1958.

Kung, Hans, *The Church.* Garden City, NY: Doubleday and Company, 1976.

Schillebeeckx, Edward, *Ministry: Leadership in the Community of Jesus Christ.* New York: Crossroad, 1984.

## The Ministry of the Laity

Banks, Robert, *All the Business of Life.* P.O. Box 320, Sutherland, NSW 2232, Australia: Albatross Books, 1987.

Diehl, William, *Thank God, It's Monday!* Philadelphia: Fortress Press, 1982.

________________, *The Monday Connection.* San Francisco: Harper and Row, 1991.

Doohan, Leonard, *The Lay Centered Church.* Minneapolis: Winston Press, 1984.

Vos, Nelvin, *Seven Days a Week.* Philadelphia: Fortress Press, 1987.

## The World Where Ministry is Lived and Practiced

Bellah, Robert N., *et al., Habits of the Heart.* Berkeley, CA: University of California Press, 1985.

________________, *The Good Society.* New York: Alfred Knopf, 1991.

Terkel, Studs, *Working: People Talk About What They Do All Day and How They Feel About What They Do.* New York: Ballantine Books, 1972.

________________, *The Great Divide: Second Thoughts on the American Dream.* New York: Avon Books, 1988.

## Educational and Liturgical Materials

Carey, George, "Values in Vocation: A Challenge for the Laity." Videotape of the Archbishop of Canterbury's keynote address and teleconference September 1992. (Available through Trinity Bookstore, 74 Trinity Place, New York, New York 10006, 1-800-551-1220.)

"A Sunday For Monday—A Guide for Ministry Sunday." Chicago: Evangelical Lutheran Church in America, Division for Congregational Life, 1990.

Droel, William L., *The Spirituality of Work: Businesspeople.* Chicago: ACTA Publications, 1991. (4848 N. Clark Street, Chicago, IL 60640-4711, 1-800-397-2282.)

Also available by same author, from same publisher: *The Spirituality of Work: Homemakers; The Spirituality of Work: Lawyers;* and *The Spirituality of Work: Teachers.*

Foley, Gerald and Schmaltz, Timothy, *Connecting Faith and Life.* Kansas City, MO: Sheed and Ward, 1987.

Kauffman, Angela, and Kauffman, David, *The Litany of Work.* Chicago: ACTA Publications, 1992.

Konieczny, Stanley J. and Pierce, Gregory F. Augustine, *For Those Who Work: Stations of the Cross.* Chicago: ACTA Publications, 1991.

Pierce, Gregory F. Augustine, ed., *Of Human Hands: A Reader in the Spirituality of Work.* Minneapolis: Augsburg, 1991.

Reber, Robert E., *Linking Faith with Daily Life: An Educational Program for Lay People.* Washington, DC: Alban Institute, 1991. (4125 Nebraska Ave. NW, Washington, D.C. 20016-2700, 202-244-7320.)

Tucker, Graham, *The Faith-Work Connection: A Practical Application of Christian Values in the Marketplace.* Toronto: Anglican Book Center, 1987. (600 Jarvis St., Toronto, Ontario, Canada M4Y 2J6, 416-924-9192.)

Vos, Nelvin, *Faith in Daily Life,* with a study guide by Carl Shankweiler. Chicago: Evangelical Lutheran Church in America, 1992. (8765 West Higgins Rd., Chicago, IL 60631, 312-380-2700.)